The Prayer Walk Guide

A Step by Step Manual for Change through Prayer

Author of the Best-Selling Book
Praying for America and the Army of God

DEBBIE JANSEN

The Prayer Walk Guide

A Step by Step Manual for Change through Prayer

by

Debbie Jansen

THE PRAYER WALK GUIDE

ISBN 978-0-9898465-5-4
Published by Christian Ministries Publishing
8710 Blitzen Rd. NW
North Canton, Ohio 44720

Acknowledgments
Every attempt has been made to credit the sources of copyrighted material used in this book. If any such acknowledgment has been inadvertently omitted or miscredited, receipt of such information would be appreciated.

Scripture references are from the following unless otherwise noted. The Ryrie Study Bible, The Holy Bible, New International Version Copyright © 1973, 1978, 1984 by International Bible Society ISBN: 0-8024-7526-4

Cover photography and design by Ken Jansen
Interior design and typeset by Ken Jansen

I would like to thank the following people

for their help in creating the

Prayer Walk Guide

Tressie Roark, Membership Administrator for Moms for America. Thank you for pointing out the need for this guide. Your ideas and insights helped create this book. Because of your faithfulness, I am sure many people will be encouraged as we work to heal our nation.

Juleen Jackson, Moms For America Senior Instructor and Advisor for Cottage Meetings. Thank you for clarification about the First Amendment to the Constitution of the United States.

Amie Williams is an Intervention specialist teacher, homeschooler, and cottage leader for Moms for America, Ohio. Thank you for your supporting research.

This book belongs to

a Prayer Warrior

Praying For My Country

"If my people, which are called by my name,
shall humble themselves, and pray,
and seek my face, and turn from their wicked ways;
then will I hear from heaven, and will forgive their sin,
and will heal their land."

2 Chronicles 7:14

"God has not given us a spirit of fear,
but of power
and of love
and of a sound mind."

2 Timothy 1:7

Table of Contents

The Importance of Prayer Walks

In Matthew chapter 6, Jesus gave a lesson on prayer, fasting, sin, and faith. His instructions were grounded in the principle that religious activities are between you and God. We do not participate to gain praise from others but rather to bring Glory to our Heavenly Father.

"But when you pray,
go into your room, close the door
and pray to your Father, who is unseen.
Then your Father, who sees what is done in secret,
will reward you."
Matthew 6:6

That verse suggests that the scriptures do not promote a prayer walk. It is essential in our study of scriptures that we look for opposites. The Bible isn't always about commandments. Most of the time, it is about God's nature vs. our heart. It is possible to have opposite scriptures about different circumstances, yet they both relate to our Father's will for us.

In Matthew 6:6, Jesus dealt with a "haughty, bragging" spirit. Jesus wanted us to concentrate on our relationship with God, not our standing in the public arena. Later in verse 16, he taught that you should wash your face and smile when fasting. Don't try to look pitiful so that others will pay attention to your fasting.

But, in Joshua 6, the Israelites did not have enough men to take the city of Jericho. God "insisted" that victory would only come if "all the armed men marched around the city for six days. Seven priests were to carry trumpets of rams horns before the Ark of Covenant. Then on the seventh day, they were to march around seven times with the priests blowing their trumpets. Finally, when the priests blew a long blast on the trumpets, everyone would shout loudly."

When the Israelites did this, they were *not* hiding in a closet. And what happened? The large walls around Jericho tumbled down, and the Israelites took the city.

In Exodus, Moses had given Pharaoh plenty of chances to let God's people go. He refused and would not allow them to leave. Finally, God told Moses to put blood on the top and sides of the doorframe of houses where anyone believed in God. This sign would save them from the Angel of Death passing through Egypt and striking down every firstborn of people and animals.

"I will bring judgment to all the gods of Egypt.
I am the Lord.
The blood will be a sign for you
on the houses where you are,
and when I see the blood,
I will pass over you.
No destructive plague will touch you
when I strike Egypt."
Exodus 12: 12-13

There are many scriptures about times requiring our prayers to be public. Jesus publicly prayed when he performed a miracle. The disciples hid in the upper room just after Jesus was crucified. Yet after the Holy Spirit came upon them, they spoke so loudly that people wondered if they were drunk.

"And they all continued in amazement
and great perplexity, saying to one another,
"What does this mean?"

"But others were jeering and saying,
"They are full of sweet wine!"
Acts 1:12

America needs people who are willing to pray in their closets. America needs people ready to march around buildings and places of evil. America needs people willing to ride by a meeting place and pray. America needs PRAYER.

The form of that prayer depends on your conviction and your group of believers.

What we do know for sure is that God always responds to the prayers of His people. When you decide to pray, God will show up. When you choose to get involved, God will be there!

Do NOT be Anxious! Do NOT be Afraid. God is with you!

A Prayer Walk has advantages over praying in your closet.

#1 Movement is powerful. When you move your body forward, your brain moves through the process of praying. The energy it takes to walk will give you a renewed passion for your prayers.

#2 Movement also keeps you focused. Often when we sit, our mind tends to wander. Sometimes our prayers are interrupted with thoughts of the day, work to be done, or how the scripture relates to our life rather than the object of our prayer.

#3 Nature is close to God. Feeling the sun, hearing the birds, noticing the wind in the trees, and smelling the flowers can give us a positive focus. After all, if God takes care of the birds, sun, wind, and flowers - why wouldn't He want to care for us and our problems?

#4 When God's nature is inspiring, we can feel connected to Him. We can imagine the people and what is going on inside the building. We can imagine their possible problems or pain. When physically related to our subject, we will pray powerful prayers.

"Again, truly I tell you that
if two of you on earth agree about anything
they ask for, it will be done for them
by my Father in heaven.
For where two or three gather in my name,
there am I with them."

Matthew 18:19 Scripture

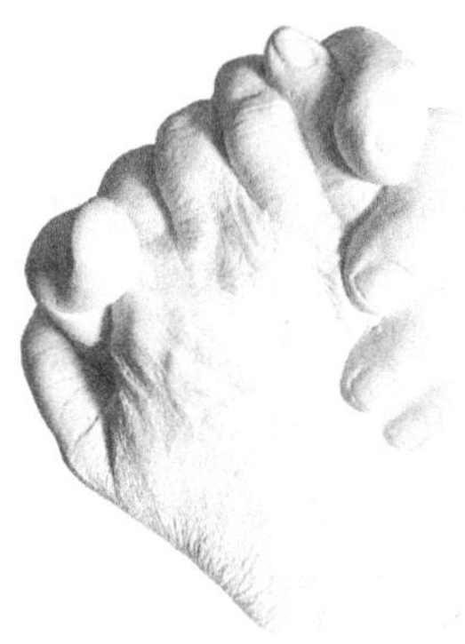

I took the above picture of a plaster mold that sits on my desk. My parents were ministers and amazing prayer warriors. One Christmas we made a plaster mold of them holding hands as they prayed for the family. When you see this picture I hope you will feel inspired to pray as they did.

God bless you as you pray!

Dear Jesus, Our Savior and Friend,

Please go with us today. We ask for your protection and wisdom. At every stop, may your Holy Spirit inspire us to pray powerful prayers that will change hearts and lives.

We love America, and we dedicate her to you. America is hurting. Our people are hurting. Children are targeted, and crime is rampant. We need your guidance and your wisdom. We need your blessings and peace. We need a revival of hearts as they turn toward you.

We are ready to work together with you for the healing of America. Teach us to be your voice, your hands, and your love. Teach us to stand for the truth. Teach us how to be mighty prayer warriors that will impact this country for you.

Thank you for the freedoms America has enjoyed. Help us to preserve Freedom, Liberty, and Virtue. Bless and protect all groups who take the time to pray for America. Bless and protect church groups, home groups, individuals, and groups like Moms For America, as we pray for our great country. Thank you for all those who are praying for America. Thank you for the moms, dads, grandparents, and others that continue to teach their family and friends about the good within America. As we join together, bless and protect the homes that are represented.

May our motto, *"In God We Trust,"* become a reality nationwide.

In the name of Jesus, we pray,

Amen

God bless you for praying for America

I have included a lot of scripture in this guide. I've also included quotes from our Presidents. I hope presidential quotes will help you realize that the strength of America has been grounded in the power of the Holy Scriptures.

Our countrymen have trusted God for protection and success. We have a history of great men who put their faith in God. May we always gather to pray for this great nation and her people.

As we bathe America in prayer, may we thank God for our many blessings, and may America continue to be the great nation God had in mind just 247 years ago.

Debbie

If you do not have a church or group to pray with, I suggest you connect with Moms For America. They are a conservative group teaching American principles and supporting prayer for our country. I am a member and I love the group. You can find them on line at www.momsforamerica.us

"No greater thing could come to our land today
than a revival of the spirit of religion — a revival
that would sweep through the homes of the nation
and stir the hearts of men and women
of all faiths to a reassertion of their belief in God
and their dedication to His will
for themselves and for their world.
I doubt if there is any problem — social, political or economic
— that would not melt away before the fire of such a spiritual
awakening."

Frankline Delano Roosevelt
32nd President of the United States of America .

A Manual for Change in America

When Jesus began His ministry, some thought He came to cause a revolution and take over the Roman government. Instead of physical fighting, Jesus taught, "I say to you who hear, Love your enemies, do good to those who hate you, bless those who curse you, pray for those who abuse you." (Luke 6:27-28)

Rather than drawing a physical sword, we, like Jesus, should turn our attention to the real cause of evil. Our enemy is not the person who has given in to evil acts but rather Satan whom that person has allowed to take over their thoughts and their lives. In other words, Jesus asked us not to hate the victim but rather to turn our eyes and attention to the oppressor. Satan is the instigator of all evil and the oppressor of all that is good.

That's why Paul wrote:

"Our struggle is not against flesh and blood, but against the rulers, against the authorities, against the powers of this dark world and against the spiritual forces of evil in the heavenly realm." (Ephesians 6:12).

This book is designed to help the body of Christ become the strongest it can be so that our prayers are powerful. It is my hope that each of us will build our spiritual muscles so we can fight against the war that invades our thinking. We must join the unseen war that rages against the evil powers of the spiritual world. The weapons we use come from God. The Bible is our constant source of instruction on how to live a life that has an impact. We grow with sustenance from the meat and the milk of the Word. Christian songs help us march even when we are exhausted. When we are frightened, sick, or worried, we call on the blood that flows from Calvary to cover and protect us. When we need comfort and peace we call on the Holy Spirit. When we are lonely we engage in spiritual fellowship. God is our never-failing friend. When we need power and strength, we have the passion of Christ. When we need vision, Jesus says, "Join me and we will change the world!

When Satan knocks on our door, we answer with a battle cry.

"I am a child of God, made in His image, redeemed by His love, accepted into His family, adorned with His crest, enlarged by His power, an heir to His throne, protected by His angels, covered with His blood, guided by His will, united in His passion and victorious by all the power of God our Father. Satan...I am your worst nightmare. Get out of my life!"

Prayer Walk Etiquette

The purpose of a prayer walk is to allow "God" to work in the lives of others. You are the instrument God works through. You are not the focus. God loves you, and wants to meet your needs, but that's for another time. Your prayer walk purpose is to ask God to move in your community and your country. You are joining with your best friend, Jesus, to make a difference in the lives of those around you.

"The LORD detests the sacrifice of the wicked,
but the prayer of the upright pleases Him."
Proverbs 15:8 NIV

When you understand that your Heavenly Father adores you and your prayers, you can relax knowing He listens to every word. He will be with you.

If you encounter an irritable anti-Christian, they should not be your focus. Linking arms with God is your purpose, and your prayer walk is your focus.

Be as inconspicuous as you can. Smile as much as possible. If you are asked to leave, smile - nod, and walk away. Never allow anyone to see you frustrated or angry. **A PRAYER walk is NOT** the place to show your frustration.

A PRAYER WALK IS all about being an instrument that God can use to leave a powerful impact on that section of town.

Remember, God is all-powerful and almighty. He knows everything and can do anything He wants. If you can pray on-site, that's great. But God doesn't need you on-site in order to answer your prayers.

Inspiration

"When Jesus had entered Capernaum,
a centurion came to him, asking for help.
"Lord", he said, "my servant lies at home paralyzed,
suffering terribly." Jesus said to him,
"Shall I come and heal him?"
The centurion relied, "Lord, I do not deserve
to have you come under my roof.
But just say the word, and my servant will be healed. For I
myself am a Man under authority,
with soldiers under me. I tell this one,
'Go', and he goes; and that one, 'Come', and he comes.
I say to my servant, 'Do this,' and he does it."
When Jesus heard this, he was amazed
and said to those following him,
"Truly I tell you, I have not found anyone
in Israel with such great faith." .....
(13)Then Jesus said to the centurion,
"Go! Let it be done just as you believed it would."
And his servant was healed at that moment."
Matthew 8:5-8 and 13

Unique and personal Prayer Walks.

By using Matthew 8:5-13, we can design different unique and personal prayer walks. Perhaps your group would like to choose from the following unique prayer walks.

#1 Your group may choose to do a traditional prayer walk by walking around a specific building or venue quietly as you pray.

#2 You can also plan a drive-by prayer. Every day a carload of members slowly drive by a specific building or area and pray.

#3 Plan a "Round About" prayer walk. Everyone in your group can pick a different building. Each person walks or drives by a specific place for a week and prays for God to intervene. Then like musical chairs, the next week, individuals swap their destinations.

#4 The "God Knows" prayer walk. Enlist someone in your group to go to different spots in town and take pictures. Have the images blown up and printed. Once a week or more, ask members to meet in a home or room in your church. Spread the pictures out on a table. Everyone can walk around the table and pray as if they were at those locations.

#5 My house is my town prayer walk. Take pictures of the places you want to use in your prayer walk. Print and place them on different doors in your home. Walk around as if you were walking through town and pray for God to intervene. You could leave them up all the time to remind you to pray.

List your ideas for a "Prayer Walk"

Prayers are powerful. Coupled with scripture, they are unbeatable. Jesus used scripture when Satan tried to tempt Him. (Luke 4:1-13)

The disciples used anointing oil when they asked for miracles. (Mark 6:13) When my children were small, I anointed the door to their rooms and prayed that God would guide and protect them as they walked under the oil. I've anointed people, pictures of people, or the map where they live. Anointing with oil is an outward expression of your prayer and God's promise to hear your prayer.

In 2nd Kings 6, Elisha caused havoc with the King of Aram who was at war with Israel. Elisha knew every move the King of Aram had planned. He passed those plans to the people of Israel. This made the King angry. He sent an army with horses and chariots to surround the city. In verse 15-17, Elisha's servant was afraid. "Don't be afraid, those who are with us are more than those who are with them." When Elisha prayed for God to open his servant's eyes, the servant saw that the hills were full of horses and chariots of fire ready to protect God's people

We are not alone! God is with us!

I believe that there are times when God requires that we act first. When He is sure we are invested in the solution- God adds his miraculous power.

I don't believe America is bad enough that destruction is on the way. I am optimistic that if we follow God's instructions to turn from our wicked ways and pray - He will heal our land.

When you approach Satan with a desire to drive him out of your town, your school, or your neighborhood, you will need power. You are fighting a spiritual war.

Notice how often God repeats in the following scripture, ***"Do NOT be afraid. Do NOT be discouraged."*** We are God's children, and he will never leave us.

"No one will be able to stand against you
all the days of your life.
As I was with Moses, so I will be with you;
I will never leave you nor forsake you.
Be strong and courageous,
because you will lead these people to inherit
the land I swore to their ancestors to give them.
Be strong and very courageous.
Be careful to obey all the law my servant Moses
gave you; do not turn from it to the right or to the left,
that you may be successful wherever you go.
Keep this Book of the Law always on your lips;
meditate on it day and night,
so that you may be careful to do everything written in it.
Then you will be prosperous and successful.
Have I not commanded you?"

"Be strong and courageous.
Do not be afraid; do not be discouraged,
for the Lord your God will be with you wherever you go."
Joshua 1:5-9

Receiving an answer to prayer
is not your only objective.
Developing a relationship with God
is your objective.

Debbie Jansen

Faith is not a one-time gift.
It is a ongoing daily fight for
spiritual dominance over our
earthly experience.
It is a moment-to-moment desire
to see God and
have Him touch our lives!

Debbie Jansen

Avoiding Dangerous Confrontations

Having Faith is refusing
to allow Satan to control us or our emotions.
We are the Children of God.
We must not give in to temptations
from Satan or evil people.
Through Jesus, we can accept the gift of power over Satan.

#1 Remember your purpose. You are there to pray against evil and for a better outcome for America. You are not there to win an argument. Sometimes after a whispered prayer, it takes days, months, or even years for the answer to arrive. Allow God time to bring about a different response.

#2 Walk away quietly if asked to leave. Your actions will determine if you have won another day of praying and the possibility that God will change everything.

#3 Do take someone that can protect your safety. If the situation escalates, moving quickly to a safe position is essential.

#4 Juleen Jackson, Moms For America Senior Instructor and Advisor for Cottage Meetings, states, "Our forefathers provided valuable protections for any free speech issue. The 1st Amendment to the Constitution guarantees the right to gather peaceably and the right to have free speech. We also have the

Inspiration

right to pray publicly. Religious liberty to faith practices can't be prohibited. It is our 1st Amendment right!"

To view all the First Amendment Fundamental Freedoms, you can visit...

https://constitution.congress.gov/browse/amendment-1/

#5 However, because we are living in a difficult time and so many people do not know the Constitution or our guaranteed rights, you must have a backup plan. Write down the number of an attorney or other official you can call if the situation escalates. Let them know ahead of time what you will be doing and why.

"It is the duty of all nations to
acknowledge the providence of
Almighty God,
to obey His will, to be grateful for His benefits,
and humbly to implore
His protection and favor."

George Washington
First President of the United States of America

YOUR CHURCH

Before your prayers reach out to others, perhaps you should pray for ***your Church*** and its impact on your community. Pray about ways your members can participate even if they don't want to walk. Giving out prayer sheets for at-home members would give your prayer walk more power. Some members could provide refreshments for those who walk or simply wait for them to return from their walk for a time of home-based prayer.

"Even those I will bring to My holy mountain,
and make them joyful in My house of prayer.
Their burnt offerings and their sacrifices
will be acceptable on My alter;
For my house will be called
a house of prayer for all the peoples."
Isaiah 56:7

Have friends from the Church write their name here when they promise to pray for you.

____

____

____

Include the following five key points when you pray.

It's essential to have a plan for your prayers. Deviation from your plan is reasonable when the Holy Spirit guides you. But, planning to pray for specific needs will keep you focused.

You can write your prayers out or simply list people and situations you want to address.

1. Pray for God to make Himself real to every member of your church. Pray that your church will be a place of Inspiration powerful prayers.

2. Pray that God will reveal the Truth to everyone. (Remember, when Truth is present, minds will change.)

3. "If you love me, obey my commandments." God loves everyone and desires that they love Him too. Pray for those who don't understand your mission.

4. Pray that God will open the eyes of everyone involved so they can see America's problems in the context of God's purpose.

____

____

____

5. Pray that everyone involved will see God's great purpose and will for their lives. May God change your church and help it become more powerful as you reach out to your community.

____

____

____

Before you leave, ask God to remove every evil spirit that may inhabit any building or site you visit.

Inspiration - Lord, Deliver us From Evil

Paul's Prayer for the Church

"For this reason, I bow my knees and pray to the Father.
It is from Him that every family in heaven
and on earth has its name.
I pray that because of the riches
of His shining-greatness,
He will make you strong with power
in your hearts through the Holy Spirit.
I pray that Christ may live in your hearts by faith.
I pray that you will be filled with love.
I pray that you will be able to understand how wide and how
long and how high
and how deep His love is.
I pray that you will know the love of Christ.
His love goes beyond anything we can understand.
I pray that you will be filled with God Himself.
God is able to do much more than we ask
or think through His power working in us.
May we see His shining-greatness in the church.
May all people in all time honor Christ Jesus.
Let it be so."

Ephesians 3: 14-21

*"I have been driven many times upon my knees
by the overwhelming conviction that I had
no where else to go.
My own wisdom and that of all about me
seemed insufficient for that day."*

Abraham Lincoln,
16th President of the United States

PRAYER WARRIORS

We have prayed for the church, and now it is time to pray for the ***PRAYER WARRIORS*** - that will be going into battle.

Gather your prayer warriors together for a preliminary meeting. Read scripture, take prayer requests, and plan for the day. The Bible encourages us to anoint those who need prayer. If you are unfamiliar with this practice, you can simply gather in a circle, hold hands and pray for those around you.

Be encouraged! Do Not Be Anxious!
Do Not Be Afraid!
God will go with you and will hear your prayers.

When we are united, and work together as one, God has promised to hear our prayers and be with us. No matter what you are praying for today you must spend time with your Heavenly Father first. Allow Him to give you the strength and wisdom you need for the day. Pray that the Holy Spirit will go before you and provide you with power. It is essential to feel the hand of God "before" you begin your walk.

"Finally, be strong in the Lord
and in his mighty power.
Put on the full armor of God,
so that you can take your stand
against the devil's schemes.
For our struggle is not against flesh and blood,
but against the rulers, against the authorities,
against the powers of this dark world
and against the spiritual forces
of evil in the heavenly realms.
Therefore put on the full armor of God,
so that when the day of evil comes,
you may be able to stand your ground,
and after you have done everything, to stand.
Stand firm then, with the belt of truth
buckled around your waist,
with the breastplate of righteousness in place,
and with your feet fitted with the readiness
that comes from the gospel of peace.
In addition to all this, take up the shield of faith,
with which you can extinguish all the
flaming arrows of the evil one.
Take the helmet of salvation and the sword of the Spirit,
which is the word of God.
And pray in the Spirit on all occasions
with all kinds of prayers and requests.
With this in mind, be alert and
always keep on praying for all the Lord's people."
Ephesians 6:10-18

Be sure and include these five key points when you pray.

1. Pray for each group member that God will give them strength, insight, wisdom, peace, and power in their prayers. Ask God to use each warrior to accomplish His will. Ask God to guide each one in the group to pray for a specific person who needs the power of God in their life.

2. Pray for God to reveal Truth to every warrior and those they pray for. The Truth will battle against evil. Don't be surprised or anxious if evil pushes back at God's people. Remember whose child you are and that God has given you power over evil. Believe it!

3. "If you love me, obey my commandments." Prayer warriors live according to God's word and believe miracles will happen. Pray that God will change lives, and expect your prayers to be answered.

4. Pray that God will open the eyes of every prayer warrior. Miracles will happen if we can grab just a glimpse God's power, purpose, and solutions. Believe in God's promises, and don't let evil steal your victory!

5. Pray that each prayer warrior will be encouraged by the power of Almighty God. That power can bring revival and peace to America. When we are determined to do our part of the plan - God will always join us by doing the things we cannot.

"And Jesus said to them, "This kind cannot
be driven out by anything but prayer."
Mark 9:29

Dear Jesus,

Please go with our prayer warriors today. Give them the wisdom of the Holy Spirit as they walk and pray. Help them to understand the problems within the places they visit. Give them discernment to know how to pray for the miracles we need. In your precious Name,

Amen.

*"We have been the recipients of the
choicest bounties of Heaven;
we have been preserved these many years
in peace and prosperity; we have grown in numbers,
wealth, and power. ... But we have forgotten God.
We have forgotten the gracious hand
which preserved us in peace and multiplied
and enriched and strengthened us,
and we have vainly imagined,
in the deceitfulness of our hearts,
that all these blessings were produced
by some superior wisdom and virtue of our own.
Intoxicated with unbroken success,
we have become too self-sufficient
to feel the necessity of redeeming and preserving grace,
too proud to pray to the God that made us."*

**Abraham Lincoln,
16th President of the United States of America**

STRONG FAITH, HOMES, AND FAMILIES

The best way for our influence to reach out and change our society is for Christians to have strong homes filled with love and the knowledge of Christ. We must petition God to bless our families with Love, Wisdom, Faith, Virtue, and a strong commitment to Liberty. America will change when we live our own lives with purpose and faith in God.

"Everyone then who hears these words of mine
and does them will be like a wise man
who built his house on the rock.
And the rain fell, and the floods came,
and the winds blew and beat on that house,
but it did not fall,
because it had been founded on the rock.
And everyone who hears these words of mine
and does not do them will be like
a foolish man who built his house on the sand.
And the rain fell, and the floods came,
and the winds blew and beat against that house,
and it fell, and great was the fall of it."
Matthew 7:24

"Start children off on the way they should go,
and even when they are old they will not turn from it."
Proverbs 22:6

After you pray for your church or group, you may want to drive through specific neighborhoods and ask God to bless those families.

Be sure and include these five key points when you pray. You can write your prayer or list people or situations you want to address.

1. Pray for God to inhabit your home and be the unseen guest in the homes of every family you know. Take the time to anoint your doorways and pray for God to bless, protect and guide those that come and go into your home.

____

____

____

2. Pray for God to reveal the Truth to every parent and every child. Truth highlights and battles against evil. Our country is filled with lies. The American Christian home is uniquely qualified to teach against those lies. Ask God to give your family members the discernment to see evil and avoid the clutches of Satan.

____

____

____

3. "If you love me, obey my commandments." A home committed to faith will always be able to see solutions that others can't. Pray for God to enter every home in America and turn hearts toward truth, freedom, and the will of God.

____

____

____

4. When God is present in the home, eyes will open so family members can see problems in the context of God's purpose. Pray that every family member will view each situation through God's eyes. Pray for God to give your home peace through doing His will.

____

____

____

5. Pray that individual family members will strive to commit their lives to God's great purpose. When family members are determined to live out God's will - amazing transformations will happen in America.

____

____

____

Make it a daily commitment to ask God to remove every evil spirit that may inhabit your home or extended family unit.

A Prayer for our Families

"Do not be anxious about anything,
but in everything by prayer and
supplication with thanksgiving
let your requests be made known to God.
And the peace of God,
which surpasses all understanding,
will guard your hearts and your minds in Christ Jesus.
Finally, brothers, whatever is true,
whatever is honorable,
whatever is just, whatever is pure,
whatever is lovely whatever is commendable,
if there is any excellence, if there is anything
worthy of praise, think about these things.
What you have learned and received
and heard and seen in me -
practice these things,
and the God of peace will be with you."
Philippians 4:6-9

"The boys (and girls) of the rising generation
are to be the men (and women)
of the next, and the sole guardians
of the principles we deliver over to them."

Thomas Jefferson,
3rd President of the United States of America

Fourth Recipient of Our Prayers

AMERICA'S CHILDREN

Our heart breaks when we hear how America's children are targeted in the most evil ways.

We must protect our Children!

Bullies attack our Christian children. The Department of Education has chosen to groom innocent children for a miserable life. Businesses, social media, Hollywood, doctors, The psychological Association, newsrooms, and even our government is comfortable with child abuse. Evil is floating over our country like a heavy dark cloud. Evil is at war, and the prize is our children's future.

We must pray for the protection of our Christian homes and our children. But, to save our country and follow God's will, we must battle Satan for the hearts and minds of "ALL" children in America and the world.

When the innocence of children is replaced with an evil agenda, those children will not have the tools needed to fight for their own survival. They become angry, lost people living dark, dysfunctional lives. We must fight for a child's right to have an innocent, safe, loving childhood.

"If anyone causes one of these little ones
—those who believe in me—to stumble,
it would be better for them to have
a large millstone hung around their neck
and to be drowned in the depths of the sea.
Woe to the world because of the things
that cause people to stumble!
Such things must come, but woe
to the person through whom they come!"
Matthew 18:6-7

Be sure and include these five key points when you pray. You can write your prayer or list people or situations you want to address.

1. Pray for God to convict abusers. I have witnessed conviction engulf wrongdoers until they had no choice but to surrender to God. Through your prayers, the Holy Spirit will fight a spiritual war to protect all of America's children. He can make himself real to every child while convicting the abuser.

____

____

____

2. Pray for God to reveal the Truth to every parent, abuser, and child in America. We must stop the evil lies that seek to enslave our children. Due to our country's lack of spiritual influence, many abusers don't see their acts as evil. Pray for God to open their eyes and convict them with truth.

____

____

____

3. God loves people, but he does NOT love evil. He wants everyone to love him, but they must turn away from their wicked ways. We must pray against all evil in America to use 2 Chronicles 7:14 to save our land.

"Jesus did say, 'If you love me,
obey my commandments.'"
(John 14:15-17)

God does not bless evil. The most loving thing we can do is pray against sin and ask God to intervene and protect our children. It is also good that we pray for the abuser to receive salvation. When their life takes a turn toward God, the abuse will stop.

Pray against the evil that would harm our children. Pray for the following areas.

____

____

____

The Health of America's Children. Evil people have made them a target. They will need God's protection from harm.

Our Children's Minds. May they be turned toward God and His commandments. Ask God to stop indoctrination.

Pray against all forms of sexual abuse, trafficking, and sexual indoctrination.

4. Pray that God will open the eyes of abusers so they can see the evil they commit. Pray that they will be disgusted by the sin of their actions. Pray that they will hear the millions of children as they cry in pain. Pray that those who want to steal our children's innocence will see that child through God's eyes.

5. Pray that abusers will see God's great purpose and plans for every little life. May they be convicted for the harm they are doing.

From the unborn to the graduating young adult, America's citizens and laws must protect and empower our children. They are our future. They will be the chosen adults leading this country into the future. They will be responsible for America's future.

____

____

____

Ask God to remove every evil spirit that may inhabit the innocent lives of our children. Ask God to shield them from those that would harm their lives.

Prayers for our Children

"Behold, children *are* a heritage from the Lord,
The fruit of the womb *is* a reward."
Psalm 127:3 (NKJV)

"Then people brought little children to Jesus
for him to place his hands on them
and pray for them. But the disciples rebuked them.
Jesus said, "Let the little children come to me,
and do not hinder them,
for the kingdom of heaven belongs to such as these."

"When he had placed his hands on them,
he went on from there."
Matthew 19:13-15

"Jesus said to his disciples:
"Things that cause people to stumble
are bound to come,
but woe to anyone through whom they come.
It would be better for them to be thrown
into the sea with a millstone tied around their neck
than to cause one of these little ones to stumble.
So watch yourselves."
Luke 17:1-3

Dear Jesus,

America is in a war with those who desire to destroy our children. I pray that every child in America will receive your protection, your guidance, and the freedom to live out your purpose for their lives. Convict and punish those that would harm any child. Convict those who are willing to ignore the pain of our children. Help us to be brave enough to fight for the innocence and safety of all children. Help us to be better parents as we raise the next generation of Christians, Patriots, and leaders.

Amen

For a more in-depth Bible study about abuse, you can order my book "Scriptures Against Abuse" on my website at

www.debbiejansen.com

*"Facts are stubborn things;
and whatever may be our wishes,
our inclination, or the dictates of our passions,
they cannot alter the state of facts
and evidence."*

John Adams,
2nd President of the United States of America

*"A thorough knowledge of the Bible
is worth more than a college education."*

Theodore Roosevelt
26th President of the United State of America

Fifth Recipient of Our Prayers

SCHOOLS, COLLEGES, DAYCARE, AND OTHER LEARNING FACILITIES

In our life, we will receive the Truth in four ways.

#1. Our parent's instructions give us the groundwork and tools to find truth as we grow. The lessons they teach us about our world will follow us into adulthood. They can change us and give us the tools for better lives.

#2. Books can change our lives like no other learning can. The three ways to commit a truth to memory are to read, write, and learn a story about it.

#3. Formal teaching, whether in our churches, schools or even at home, can present facts and teach the ability to search for Truth using critical thinking. It's crucial to receive Truth in our churches and school settings.

#4. We can learn valuable lessons through our failures and life experiences. Life experiences are harsh teachers, but they often provide determination and practical information.

God instructs Christian parents to protect their children. We must continually pray for our public schools to change. We must care about the children who are trapped in a bad situation. And we must be willing to take our children out of those schools if necessary.

"My people are destroyed for lack of knowledge;
because you have rejected knowledge,
I reject you from being a priest to me.
And since you have forgotten
the law of your God,
I also will forget your children."
Hosea 4:6

Be sure and include these five key points when you pray. You can write your prayer or list people or situations you want to address.

1. We must pray for God to convict public teachers who wish to change our society by promoting immoral cultural practices in the classroom. Children are innocent. They naturally believe adults have authority over them. We must pray for a safe environment for our children. We need good teachers who will protect the innocence of our children and support the parent's desires for Virtues, Liberty, Respect and Faith-based morals. Ask the Holy Spirit to flow through every classroom

and protect our children. May God help parents with a plan when it is necessary to take their children out of the system.

2. Pray for God to reveal theTruth to every parent who has a child in public education. "Let Truth be Revealed" must be our daily prayer. We can't protect our children without the truth about classroom activities. Not only do we need Truth for our parents, but our children need the power and ability to stand for Truth in the classroom.

3. Evil exists in every area of our society. Pray that God's power will overcome evil in our public schools and higher education. Evil prospers when lies are present. We need God's power to rebuke and dispose of all evil in our learning facilities. Pray that all classrooms and libraries will reject the lies of satan. God does not bless evil. Ask God to remove the evil that would harm our children.

4. Pray that God will convict teachers, principals, and school board members trying to steal our children's innocence. May they feel God's convicting power every time they walk through the doors of their school. May they feel uncomfortable and unable to harm our children. Pray that as Truth is revealed, everyone involved will be disgusted by sin. Pray that every teacher will see each student through God's eyes.

5. Pray that everyone involved in education will see God's purpose and will for every life. Pray that American teachers and educational employees will seek to protect and empower our children from the unborn to the graduating adult. They are our future. America can only be strong when our children are protected and guided by God's laws.

Dear Jesus,

We ask you to eliminate every evil spirit that seeks to inhabit the innocent minds of our children. If they must attend public school, give them discernment against evil. Walk with them and protect them. Place a bubble of your love, wisdom, and power around them. If any teacher seeks to hurt them, let that truth be known to every parent. Give each parent a bold and unyielding spirit to help them protect our children. Give our children the power to resist Satan and his evil ways. In your precious name,

Amen

"It is impossible to rightly govern a nation without God and the Bible."

George Washington,
First President of the United States of America

"Before any man can be considered
as a member of civil society,
he must be considered as a subject
of the Governor of the Universe.
And to the same Divine Author
of every good and perfect gift
we are indebted for all those privileges
and advantages, religious as well as civil,
which are so richly enjoyed in this favored land."

James Monroe
5th President of the United States of America

Sixth Recipient of Our Prayers

Federal and Local Governments

Federal and local governments were created to bring *"order"* to our country. God loves order. Everything He created is filled with order and purpose. Our forefathers understood that the entire system falls apart when the government takes over God's job.

"When the righteous thrive, the people rejoice;
when the wicked rule, the people groan.
A man who loves wisdom brings joy to his father,
but a companion of prostitutes squanders his wealth.
By justice a king gives a country stability,
but those who are greedy for bribes tear it down."
Proverbs 29:2-4

"I urge, then, first of all, that petitions,
prayers, intercession and thanksgiving
be made for all people for kings and
all those in authority,

that we may live peaceful and quiet lives
in all godliness and holiness."
1Timothy 2:1-2

There are also many scriptures about accepting the rule of law over you. The one scripture that helps us decide how to deal with our government is Matthew 22:15-21. We are God's children. We belong to Him. We must and should obey all laws of this country - until those laws take us away from God. That is when we must stand on God's word and His law. That is what has made this a wonderful country.

The men who wrote our laws believed our rights come from God. Our laws reflect all the intentions of Freedom, Liberty, Faith, and Virtue. For years we have been able to live peaceably with others because we observed the laws of God.

"Then the Pharisees went out and laid plans
to trap him in his words. They sent their disciples
to him along with the Herodians. "Teacher," they said,
"we know that you are a man of integrity
and that you teach the way of God
in accordance with the truth.
You aren't swayed by others,
because you pay no attention to who they are.
Tell us then, what is your opinion?
Is it right to pay the imperial tax to Caesar or not?"
But Jesus, knowing their evil intent, said,
"You hypocrites, why are you trying to trap me?"

"Show me the coin used for paying the tax."
They brought him a denarius, and he asked them,
"Whose image is this? And whose inscription?"
"Caesar's," they replied.
Then he said to them, "So give back to Caesar
what is Caesar's, and
to God what is God's."
Matthew 22 15:21

Be sure and include these five key points when you pray. You can write your prayer or list people or situations you want to address.

1. Pray for God to convict government officials who break our laws. Pray that their evil deeds will be revealed.

___

___

___

2. Pray for God to reveal the Truth about every government employee and politician. Ask God to continue to show the truth in all legal matters. May your prayers petition the Holy Spirit to fight against all lies floating through public communications, radio, television, internet and social media. We need the Truth of God to prevail over evil so we can have the freedom to live godly lives.

___

3. God loves people, but he does NOT love evil. Ask God to eliminate all evil attempts to destroy America, her Christian heritage. We must pray against evil in America to use 2 Chronicles 7:14 to save our land. God does not bless evil. If we want this country to succeed, we must pray against satan and reject his plans at every point.

4. Pray that God will open the eyes of those who want to change America into a nation without God. Pray that as truth is revealed, evildoers will be disgusted by sin. Pray that God's people will rise, do the right thing, and ensure that revival comes to America.

5. Pray that all Americans will return to the beliefs of our founding fathers. On March 21, 1630, Puritan John Winthrop's lecture, *A Model of Christian Charity,* stated that America would be seen "as a city upon a hill" and "the eyes of all people are upon us." In other words, if the Puritans failed to keep their covenant

with God, all the world would see their sins and faults. He continued, "So that if we shall deal falsely with our God in this work we have undertaken and so cause him to withdraw his present help from us, we shall be made a story and a byword through the world."

We must take our country back!

____

____

____

America has been through dark days due to the sins and criminal acts of flawed men. She has suffered attacks, wars, riots, plots, assassinations, depressions, disease, and conspiracies. But praise God, America has also enjoyed the blessings of God for her goodness, her charity, and her willingness to stand against evil. America is blessed by the millions of praying Christians who make up the body of Christ.

A Prayer For Our Government

Dear Jesus,

Thank you for our forefathers who sought you while organizing this country. Thank you for leading men to design a God-fearing country that cares about its citizens.

America has lost its way. We are struggling to be the country we once were. We beg you not to bring judgment on America but instead to bring guidance. Allow your Holy Spirit to flow through every government office and touch the lives of every politician.

Fill our government offices with men and women who lean on you for guidance and inspiration. Bring about a new era of safety, prosperity, peace, and a deep love for you. We ask all these things in your name,

Amen

*"The reason that Christianity
is the best friend of government
is because Christianity
is the only religion
that changes the heart."*

*Thomas Jefferson,
3rd President of the United States of America*

Seventh Recipient of Our Prayers

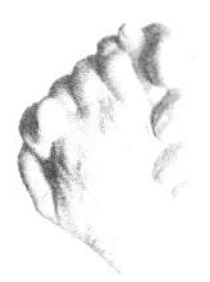

Our Town "Welcome to _______________ sign.

Ask your group to go to the edge of town, or take a picture of your boundary town sign. Our prayers aren't desperate until our needs hit home. I know many wonderful Christians who ignored the evils of abortion until the number of babies murdered ran into the millions. Today many wonderful Christians turn their heads rather than discuss the evils of our current culture wars. Yet, when a granddaughter chooses abortion or a nephew decides to transition because a school teacher told him to - they become activists.

Let's start our work by anointing the town sign and praying for all our borders. Our powerful prayers will help us fight for our rights and faith one small town at a time.

"For this reason, since the day we heard about you,
we have not stopped praying for you.
We continually ask God to fill you
with the knowledge of his will through
all the wisdom and understanding
that the Spirit gives,
so that you may live a life worthy of the Lord"

"and please him in every way: bearing fruit
in every good work, growing in the knowledge of God,
being strengthened with all power
according to his glorious might
so that you may have great endurance and patience,
and giving joyful thanks to the Father,
who has qualified you to share in the inheritance
of his holy people in the kingdom of light.
For he has rescued us from the dominion of darkness
and brought us into the kingdom of the Son he loves,
in whom we have redemption,
the forgiveness of sins."
Colossians 1: 9-14

Be sure and include these five key points when you pray. You can write your prayer or list people or situations you want to address.

1. Pray for God to flood your town with the spirit of His holy love. May all your cities and townships feel a great desire to know Jesus. Once they have met the Savior, all things will change.

____

____

____

2. Pray for God to reveal the Truth in your town. May God reveal all evil actions so they can be eliminated. Pray for God to

open the eyes of every citizen of your town so that you may go forward and make your city the best it can be.

---

3. God loves your town, but He does *not* love evil. Pray that your citizens will turn from their wicked ways so God can heal and prosper your town.

---

4. Pray that God will open the eyes of every person in your town so they can see how much better life will be without evil. Ask God to stir the hearts of everyone and cause a great revival in your city.

---

5. Pray that every person in your town will see God's great purpose for their family and life. We know that when we all work toward God's goal, we are more successful and happier.

A Prayer For Our Town

Dear Jesus,

We need your help and your blessing. We need you to inspire us to make our town better. We are suffering, and we need guidance. Give our people wisdom. Give our citizens truth and faith. Give our children a future full of hope and peace. Teach us how to guide our families so we can live according to your purpose and your will. Bless us, dear Jesus.
Amen

"The Lord bless you and keep you;
The Lord make His face shine upon you,
And be gracious to you;
The Lord lift up His countenance upon you,
And give you peace."
Numbers 6:24-26

*"Each day millions of our citizens
approach our Maker on bended knee,
seeking His grace and giving thanks
for the many blessings He bestows upon us."*

George W Bush
43rd President of the United States of America

Eighth Recipient of our Prayers

THE LOCAL BUSINESS

One of God's greatest blessings is an honest, God-fearing business leader. Local communities need local businesses that serve individual families. They are the heartbeat of our towns. It is important to let them know how much we appreciate and need their services. It is also very essential to pray for them and to help them find Salvation. Everyone wins when they view their business as a purpose within the body of Christ.

"Remember this: Whoever sows sparingly
will also reap sparingly, and whoever sows generously
will also reap generously.
Each of you should give what you have decided
in your heart to give, not reluctantly or under compulsion,
for God loves a cheerful giver.
And God is able to bless you abundantly,
so that in all things at all times,
having all that you need,
you will abound in every good work."
2 Corinthians 9: 6-8

Be sure and include these five key points when you pray. You can write your prayer or list people or situations you want to address.

1. Pray for God to inspire business within your community. Pray that God-loving men and women will fulfill the needs of your citizens.

____

____

____

2. Business leaders must pray and watch the bottom line to be successful. But Christian leaders will always strive to trust God and pray for pray every customer. Pray that God's balance sheet will be used for every business.

____

____

____

3. Mention your favorite businesses in your prayers. Ask God to give them honest employees. Ask God to help them stand against evil and refuse to do anything that isn't pleasing to God. Ask God to give them strength and wisdom.

____

____

____

____

____

4. Ask God to protect your town against businesses promoting evil practices that will harm your people. Ask God to keep satanic groups, drug dealers, prostitution, gangs, and other evil companies out of your town. Ask God to protect your city against evil forces.

____

____

____

5. Pray that every business leader will see the town as God sees it. Pray that they will work to keep your town clean, safe, and prosperous.

____

____

____

A Prayer For Our Local Businesses

Dear Jesus,

Thank you for the businesses and business leaders we have. Please continue to bless our town with new Christian business leaders. We need a safe and secure city so we can worship you. We need a town that allows our church to grow and fulfill the great commission. We need a town that will allow each family to raise our children and live our lives the way you want us to live.

We can't be prosperous without local businesses investing in our people. We ask you to allow our local business leaders to feel your love and to be drawn to you. Protect them and give them the strength they need to fight against evil. Please bless our community with more Christian business leaders as we go forward.

Amen

*"The spirit of man is more important
than mere physical strength,
and the spiritual fiber of a nation than its wealth.
The Bible is endorsed by the ages.
Our civilization is built upon its words.
In no other book is there such a collection
of inspired wisdom, reality, and hope."*

*Dwight D. Eisenhower,
34th President of the United States of America*

HOSPITALS, DOCTORS, CLINICS, MEDICAL SERVICES

"He said to her,
"Daughter, your faith has healed you.
Go in peace and be freed
from your suffering."
Mark 5:34

It would be wonderful if every illness came with a quick prayer and complete healing. Unfortunately, even in Jesus' day, some people were not healed.

We need talented, kind, and trustworthy medical care. While it is our responsibility to try to live clean healthy lives, at some point, all of us will need the supervision of a good doctor. I pray that God will infuse our country with men and women who understand their limits and trust God to aid their work when we need their help.

Be sure and include these five key points when you pray. You can write your prayer or list people or situations you want to address.

1. Pray that God will bless our nation with men and women who take their medical jobs seriously. Pray that they will not withhold medical help for financial gain. We must also pray they will refuse to do unnecessary or evil procedures for financial gain.

____

____

____

2. Many people are hurt or even killed because a medical professional is evil or doesn't care about the individual's life. Pray that God will reveal the Truth and that professionals will once again have to live up to a code of ethics.

____

____

____

3. Unfortunately, America has become a country where the medical profession is aiding in the evil practices of the present culture wars. Pray that God will intervene and remove the desire to participate in procedures or methods that harm all Americans - especially Christians. Make a list of the evils you see and pray against them.

____

____

____

____

____

4. America has many great doctors. Many of those doctors are Christians, and they are alarmed at the abusive procedures that are happening. Pray for God to strengthen and protect those medical professionals who speak out and sound the alarm about evil practices. Pray that God will open public eyes to the dangers within our medical communities.

5. Pray that everyone in America will understand how critical medical professionals are to America's success. Weak and sick people can't move a country forward. Pray that God will continue to bless this nation with medical professionals who are only concerned about helping every citizen in America.

A Prayer For America's Medical Community

Dear Jesus,

Anyone who trains for a medical degree has chosen a "Godly" profession. Their kindness and desire to help the injured is very close to your kindness toward us. Thank you for their service to our communities. We know there are some who do not see these jobs as important. Please touch their hearts with your Holy Spirit so they will turn to you. Those who are working to be your hands and to help us heal, please strengthen and guide them. Give them wisdom and a desire to protect us from harm as well as guide us to physical and mental health. Amen

"Heroism is not only in the man,
but in the occasion."

Calvin Coolidge,
30th President of the United States of America

"God who gave us life gave us liberty.
Can the liberties of a nation be secure
when we have removed a conviction
that these liberties are the gift of God?
Indeed I tremble for my country
when I reflect that God is just,
that His justice cannot sleep forever."

Thomas Jefferson,
3rd President of the United States of America
(quote inscribed on the Jefferson Memorial)

Tenth Recipient of Our Prayers

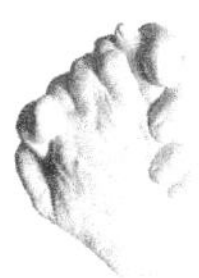

POLICE, ARMED SERVICES, FIRE DEPARTMENT, 911 RESPONDERS, AND ANYONE WHO RUSHES INTO DANGER.

Praying for those who protect me or come to my rescue on my worst day is one of the hardest prayers I pray. Anyone in that position may put their life on the line at any moment. They drive at unimaginable speeds. They fight to control the area and the situation. They must have a quick response to save lives. How do they do that? What is going through their mind? It humbles me to tears.

Additionally, they don't even know me, yet they are willing to die or run into dangerous situations to save me. I am broken and grateful for their service.

When I hear about a fallen policeman, EMT, fireman, or serviceman, I instantly hope and pray they made Heaven. When I hear a firetruck go by or an EMT, I pray that they arrive safely, and for the people that may be hurt. I've been in a position where I needed an EMT to administer safe and quick help to keep me alive. I thank God for them. I have friends who are responders, and most days, they are put in dangerous positions to save those who call for help. My State Trooper friend relays stories that will break your heart.

May we never forget to pray for and thank those that are willing to die to keep us safe. They indeed are a gift from God.

"My command is this:
Love each other as I have loved you.
Greater love has no one than this:
to lay down one's life for one's friends.
You are my friends if you do what I command."
John 15: 13-14

Be sure and include these five key points when you pray. You can write your prayer or list people or situations you want to address.

1. No one wants to call the police for help only to discover they are the abuser, not the protector. Pray that God will convict anyone who should not be in that position. Pray that God will reveal the Truth, and the person will leave the force.

____

____

____

2. Pray for the safety and wisdom of those who *"do"* want to protect you and your home. Pray that God will send his Holy Angels to help them in their work and to protect them and their families.

3. If America is ever going to turn around, we need brave men and women willing to enforce our laws. They will require wisdom and strength to get the job done. And, they will need the power of God in their own lives. Pray for their Salvation and their protection. Anyone in the positions we've listed will need God's power to succeed and stay healthy.

4. When our safety experts, police, and armed services see each citizen as God does, they will be at their best. They will protect us with honor and with God's passion. Christian men and women who serve others have the full force of God behind them. Pray for a revival in those positions.

5. Pray that everyone who serves in security and safety will see their community with God's eyes. May they feel compassion as well as a sense of justice. Pray that God will help each person to fulfill God's purpose for their lives.

____

____

____

A Prayer For Our Medical Community

Dear Jesus,

Thank you for every man and woman who is ready to help us on our worst days. Thank you for every police unit that rushes to an emergency. Thank you for the men and women who quickly run toward danger rather than running away. Thank you for every serviceman willing to die so this country can be safe and free. We are truly blessed to have these people in our lives.

Please eliminate those who do not have our good at heart. Convict those who would do evil. Reveal the Truth when our community is being hurt.

Please protect, guide, and prosper all those who keep us safe.

Amen

____

____

____

____

____

"I do believe in Almighty God!
And I believe also in the Bible...
Let us look forward to the time
when we can take the flag of our country
and nail it below the Cross, and there let it wave
as it waved in the olden times,
and let us gather around it and inscribed for our motto:
"Liberty and Union, one and inseparable, now and forever,"
and exclaim, Christ first, our country next!"

Andrew Johnson,
17th President of the United States of America

Eleventh Recipient of Our Prayers

ANY PLACE WHERE PEOPLE GATHER

Humans need fellowship. We crave the fellowship of God and the friendship of other humans. We need to react with others to be mentally healthy. We need to laugh and have good experiences. We need restful time to feel inspired to continue our purpose and work.

Even Jesus talked about the advantages of restful interaction.

"Then, because so many people were coming
and going that they did not even have a chance to eat,
he said to them, "Come with me by yourselves
to a quiet place and get some rest."
Mark 6:31

My Dad used to quote the King James version by saying, "Come ye apart and rest a while, or you will come apart!"

Unfortunately, our country has become the "fun nation" of the world. Satan has used the idea of getting rest to advance his evil distractions. A simple day at the park with your children can become dangerous if a sexual predator lurks around. Joining a fun group can quickly turn into an abusive problem. Too many towns are invaded by strip clubs, drug houses, and other gathering places that do not inspire our citizens for good.

There is good news.

"Verily I say unto you,
Whatsoever ye shall bind on earth
shall be bound in heaven:
and whatsoever ye shall loose on earth
shall be loosed in heaven.
Again I say unto you,
That if two of you shall agree on earth
as touching any thing that they shall ask,
it shall be done for them of my Father
which is in heaven.
For where two or three are gathered
together in my name,
there am I in the midst of them."
Matthew 18:18-20

Matthew 18:18-20 is a powerful verse! It gives us the power to fix all the problems contained in this book. We have the power to bind evil here on earth. Through our prayers, we have the power to ask God to stop the evil that surrounds us. Yes, we pray for His will, but we are confident that if we pray for the things He desires, He will answer.

Do Not Be Anxious. Do Not Be Afraid.

We can pray with confidence that God will protect any gathering place. We can pray with power that any evil will be stopped and bound here on earth.

As I write this, I am encouraged to know that God's people will go out and pray for God to heal our land. There is nothing in life more powerful than the prayers of God's people.

Be sure and include these five key points when you pray. You can write your prayer or list people or situations you want to address.

1. Pray for God to send His Holy Spirit to every gathering place in your town and America. May the Holy Spirit convict anyone who would bring evil acts that into that gathering place. May those that gather together feel the presence of God in that place.

____

____

____

2. Pray for God to reveal the Truth about evil to everyone in the gathering place. Too many children and adults are innocently drawn into danger when visiting a gathering place. Pray that God will protect innocent lives.

____

____

3. God loves people, but he does NOT love evil. Not every gathering place is good for us. Pray against and bind up the evil that is present in some spaces. Make a list of the areas in your town that need protection by the Holy Spirit or destruction by the hand of God. Prayer will clean up our cities.

4. Pray with your church membership about hosting a positive gathering place that can also witness to those in your town who are lonely and need fellowship.

5. Pray that the leaders in your town will decide to make every gathering place a safe space for its citizens. Getting rid of questionable places will provide safety for everyone.

Ask God to remove every evil spirit that may inhabit the gathering places in your town.

A Prayer For Your People

Dear Jesus,

Thank you for your love when you created us. You make our lives extraordinary. Thank you for being our friend and our Savior.

We ask you now to give our town safe places to rest and rebuild our strength. Inhabit our city with your love and your Holy Spirit. May we all find peace and rest because you are with us. Guide us, and please help us rebuild our country to be *One Nation Under God, with Liberty and Justice for all.*

Amen

More Places To Pray

There is no way I could predict the places you might want to include in a Prayer Walk. I've included the most obvious. Use the following pages to record your ideas for places to pray.

Write down your concerns for people or places not included in this book. Be sure to include your own scriptures, thoughts, and quotes. Being specific will help you pray powerful prayers for your community and America.

I am so proud of you and your group for taking on this exercise. God bless you for your desire to pray for America and her people.

A PRAYER FOR THE NATION

"Almighty God,
You have given us this good land for our heritage.
We humbly ask You that we may always prove ourselves
a people mindful of Your favor and glad to do Your will.
Bless our land with honorable endeavor,
sound learning and pure manners.
Save us from violence, discord, and confusion,
from pride and arrogance, and from every evil way.
Defend our liberties and fashion into one united people
the multitude brought here out of many nations
and tongues.
Endow with the Spirit of wisdom those to whom
in your Name we entrust the authority of government,
that there may be justice and peace at home,
and that through obedience to Your law
we may show forth Your praise
among the nations on earth.
In time of prosperity fill our hearts
with thankfulness, and in the day of trouble
do not allow our trust in You to fail.
Amen"

Thomas Jefferson,
3rd President of the United States

Debbie's Published books

Praying for America and the Army of God

Scriptures Against Abuse

Minutes of Faith - Podcast Devotions Journal Season #1

Cookie Swap Survival Guide 2022

The Cookie Swap

"Revised" Discipline Exposed -
Surviving Fried Worms and Flying Mudballs

Coming Soon….

The Penny System -
A Behavior Modification program for children

The Lighter Side of Chaos

Why Children Believe -
How to teach your child your faith

Debbie Jansen holds a degree in psychology and a minister's license. She received the 1999 Alumni Association President's Award from Evangel University for her work with The Family Training Center.

For thirty years, Debbie has taught and counseled those who struggle with relationships and spiritual issues. Debbie has held family conferences and taught on television and in videos.

Please visit Debbie's website for more information or to schedule a speaking engagement.
www.debbiejansen.com

Made in the USA
Columbia, SC
12 May 2024